WITHDRAWN

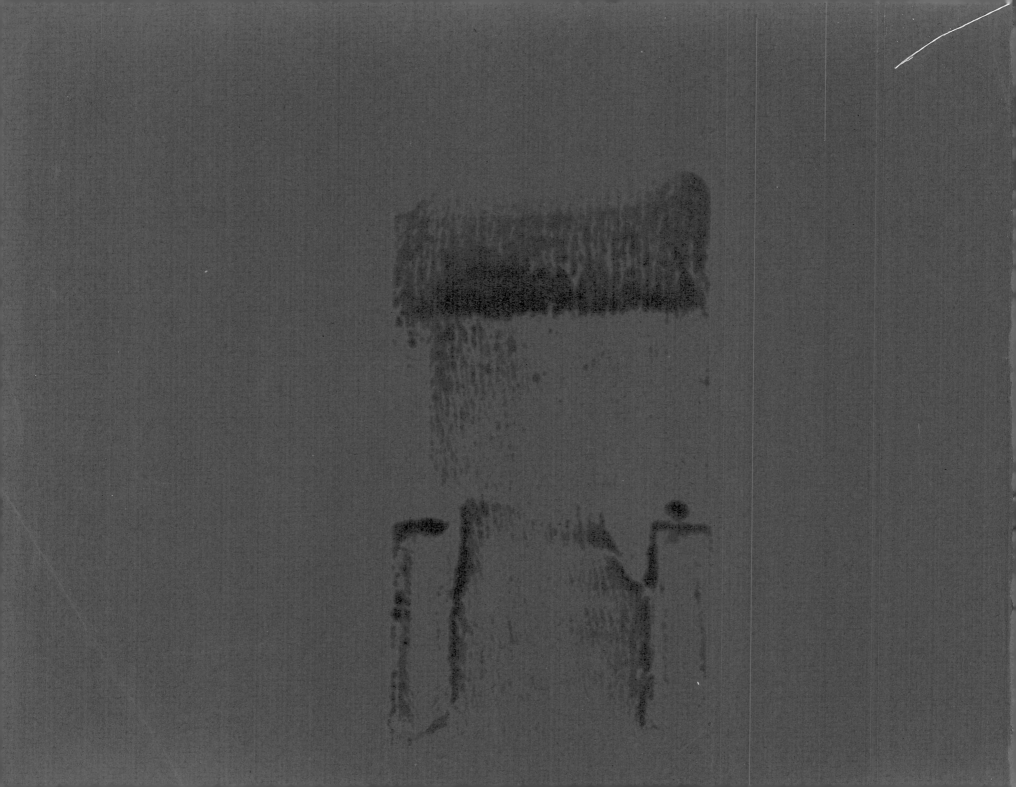

ELLIS ISLAND

Acknowledgements and Credits

Much appreciation and thanks are extended to the following for use of their material; The National Archives, Library of Congress, The Department of Immigration and Naturalization and the National Park Service. Also I would like to mention the kind assistance given to me by the Daughters of the American Revolution.

I would like to thank Mr. Willard Heaps for the use of his extensive research material and his most useful suggestions.

Most of all I would like to mention National Park Service Ranger W. Pingree Crawford without whose help and assistance this project would have been impossible, and his family whose hospitality made the project wholly enjoyable.

Wilton S. Tifft

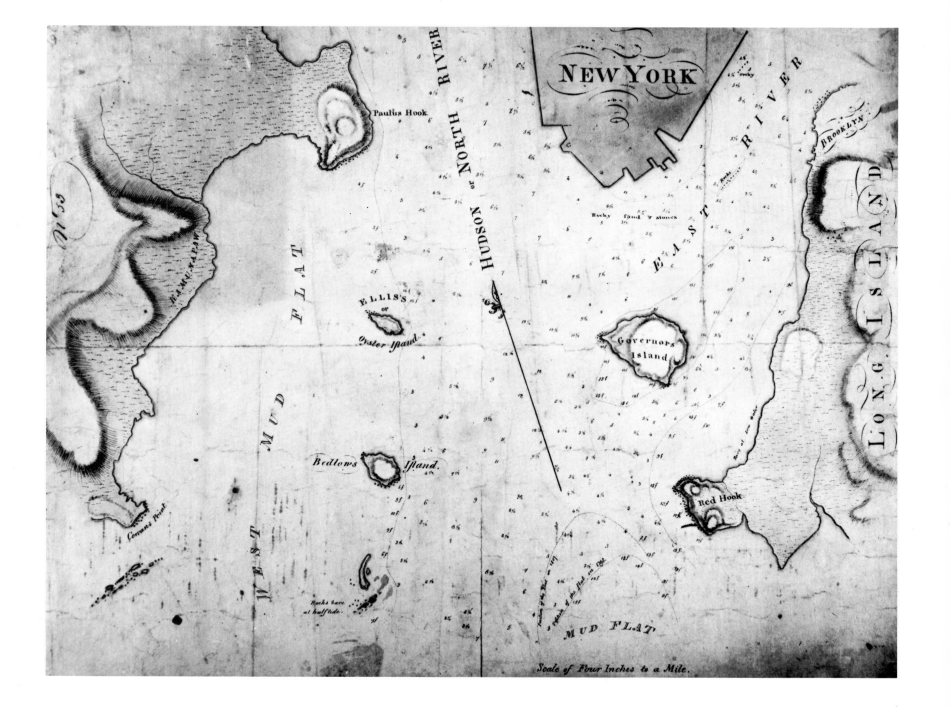

NEW YORK

Paulus Hook

HUDSON or NORTH RIVER

RIVER

BROOKLYN

Rocky sand & stones

EAST

LONG ISLAND

KAMURAPOW

FLAT

ELLIS'S
or
Oyster Island

Governors
Island

MUD

WEST

Bedlows Island.

Red Hook

Cowans Point

Rocks bare
at halftide.

MUD FLAT

Scale of Four Inches to a Mile.

PHOTOGRAPHY WILTON TIFFT **TEXT** THOMAS DUNNE **DESIGN** MILA MACEK

ELLIS ISLAND

W. W. NORTON & COMPANY INC.   NEW YORK

Published simultaneously in Canada by George J. McLeod Limited, Toronto   Printed in the United States of America   *1234567890*

to Suzanne

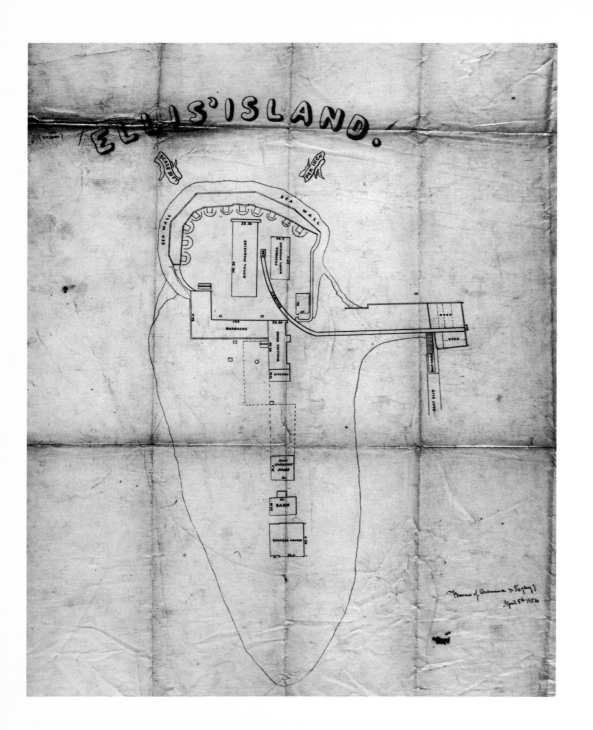

The Mohegan Indians named it *Kioshk,* or "Gull Island", after its only inhabitants—the numerous seagulls which fed on the plentiful oysters in its banks. It is doubtful that Henry Hudson took much notice of the tiny mudbank when in 1609 he sailed the *Half Moon* up the river which was to bear his name. If he took the trouble to look, he most certainly found it unattractive. Almost submerged at high tide, the four flat acres of sand and oyster shells were without fresh water, vegetation or animal life. During the century and a half after Hudson's voyage, the island acquired several names. The Dutch profitably exploited the rich oyster beds along its shore, and appropriately enough, referred to it as "Oyster Island" or "Little Oyster Island." Throughout the eighteenth century, the English often designated it "Bucking Island", an appellation of obscure origin.

In 1757, the Common Council of New York City selected a committee "to view and examine Bucking Island, whether it be fit for a pest house." The site was found unacceptable and nearby Bedloe's (now Liberty) Island was purchased the next year. A use for Oyster Island was finally found in 1765 when it was chosen as the location for the execution of a notorious pirate named Anderson. In his *Memoirs of the Rev. John Henry Livingston,* Alexander Gunn tells the story of Anderson's piracy during a voyage from New York to the Caribbean early in 1765:

When the voyage was nearly completed, two of the crew made an attempt one night to seize the vessel; and, in the prosecution of their diabolical design, all on board, except a little boy, perished by their hands. After perpetrating the horrible deed, they gave themselves up to intoxication, and in this state . . . they ordered the boy to row them . . . [to nearby St. Thomas, Virgin Islands].

Anderson's partner in crime was captured on St. Eustatius and broken on the wheel, while Anderson was taken on St. Thomas and returned to New York for trial. He was found guilty and "executed on an island in the Bay, near the city, which, from that circumstance, has ever since been called Anderson's or Gibbet Island."

Gibbet Island was the site of execution of a number of pirates for seventy-five years after Anderson's death. In 1769, a pirate named Andrews reportedly "was hung long in irons, just above Washington Market and was then taken to Gibbet Island and suspended there." The most famous execution on the island took place in April, 1831. George Gibbs and Thomas Wansley were convicted of piracy and brought to Gibbet Island for execution. The two tried in vain to speak to the crowd, "but were prevented from being heard by the clamorous tumult of the multitude." The April 23, 1831 issue of *The Mercantile Advertiser* reported that:

The concourse of spectators was immense, the little island was crowded with men and women and children—and on the waters around, were innumerable boats, laden with passengers, from the steamboat and schooner, down to the yawl and canoe. One or two boats were upset, but no lives were lost.

The first owner of what was ultimately called "Ellis Island" was Michel Paauw. For "certain cargoes, or parcels of goods," he purchased Oyster Island from the Indians in 1630, along with Staten Island and a large part of the Jersey coast. His short-lived colony of Pavonia was the first European settlement in what was to become New Jersey. In his whimsical *Knickerbocker's History of New York*, Washington Irving describes Paauw as "patroon of Gibbet Island," and claims that "his standard was . . . a huge Oyster recumbent upon a sea-green field."

Ownership of the island changed hands several times after the British took New Amsterdam. For a period of almost 50 years, no known owner can be found in city tax records, and for most of the eighteenth century the island was uninhabited. Although it is unclear how he came into possession of it, Samuel Ellis offered for sale in 1785 "That pleasant situated Island, called OYSTER ISLAND . . . together with all its improvements, which are considerable also, a parcel of spars . . . timber fit for . . . building docks; and a few barrels of excellent shad and herrings, and others of an inferior quality fit for

shipping . . . a quantity of twine . . . also a large Pleasure Sleigh, almost new."

Whether Ellis sold his herrings and sleigh is unknown, but he was certainly unable to sell Oyster Island, because it was included with his property when he died in 1794. Ellis' will contained a curious stipulation: "I do will and bequeath unto the child that Catherine Westervelt (his daughter) is now pregnant with, should it be a son, Oyster Island, commonly known as Ellis' Island, with all the buildings thereon." He further specified that his grandson-to-be should be christened Samuel Ellis, and, should the child be a girl, the property was to be divided among his granddaughters. Catherine obediently gave birth to a son and named him after her father, but the infant died several years later, and the family sold the island to John A. Berry for $3,200. Although the land passed from the Ellis family, the name "Ellis Island" remained, and by the middle of the nineteenth century was the only designation for the property.

The international tensions produced by the Napoleonic Wars made Ellis Island a potentially important strategic location. For a twenty-year period Americans expected to be drawn into a conflict with England or France. In 1794, Secretary of War Henry Knox sent Charles Vincent to New York to plan the defense of the city. Vincent proposed the construction of batteries on Bedloe's, Governor's and Oyster Islands (see map). His report noted: "After Bedloe's, and on the same side of the channel, we find a very low island (Oyster Island) which its proximity to the city, to Bedloe's and Governor's Islands, renders it infinitely precious."

In April, 1794, the city deeded Bedloe's Island and the "soil from high to low water

mark around the said Island called Ellis's Isle" to the state for necessary fortifications. The state appropriated $100,000 to strengthen harbor defenses, and in 1798, the threat of war with France goaded the legislature into providing an additional sum of $150,000. A barracks able to "accommodate one company of soldiers" was finished in Ellis Island in the same year, and the island was used as the military recruiting headquarters for New York City. Apparently, some of the volunteers found military life too harsh, and notices of desertions were not uncommon in city newspapers. A typical one, published in 1798, read:

Ten Dollars Reward, Is offered for the apprehending of Thomas Ryne, of the Corps of Artillerists and Engineers, who deserted from the Rendezvous on Ellis Island. He is a native of Ireland, about thirty years of age, five feet six inches and a half, of a dark complexion, slovenly habit, and indolent deportment, has dark hair and blue eyes.
D. Hale, Lieut. in said Corps.

English Family - SS "Adriatic" - Apr. 17 - '08.

B.G. Phillips

8 Orphan children — Mothers killed in Russian Massacre — Oct. 1905.
"SS" "Caronia" May 8 - '08.

In February, 1800, New York State gave Governor's and Bedloe's Islands to the federal government. Ellis Island was also given to the United States, but this land was only up to the high water mark, and it was clear that the remainder of the island was private property. In the years prior to the War of 1812, well over $1,000,000 was spent on fortifications in New York harbor, and on Ellis Island there were quarters for troops, casements, parapets and gun batteries.

The government's lack of a title to Ellis Island severely handicapped further efforts to fortify the position. In 1807, the War Department recognized that "a purchase should be made of the part now belonging to citizens," since it was apparent that the installation on Ellis Island was "occupied merely by the permission of the owner." The state appointed a special jury to determine the value of the land, and it priced the island at $10,000. Colonel Williams, who was in charge of preparing the defenses, was shocked by this seemingly excessive price. "The jury are acknowledged to be of the most respectable kind and generally esteemed good judges of property," he wrote to the Secretary of War, Henry Dearborn, "but in this instance they have estimated capabilities instead of real estate, taking into consideration the advantages of setting fish nets on the flats all around, letting rakes to the oystermen, and keeping a house of entertainment for all these amphibious customers." Despite the high price, the War Department authorized New York State to purchase the property, and in June of 1808, the state was reimbursed and the title to Ellis Island passed to the federal government.

The forts in New York harbor saw no action during the War of 1812, though both Ellis and Bedloe's Islands were used to house British prisoners of war. As many as 180 American troops were crowded onto Ellis Island, and the works were christened Fort Gibson, after an American officer killed in the battle of Fort Erie. The state and federal money spent on Fort Gibson, Governor's Island and Bedloe's Island was not wasted—the excellent defenses of the harbor almost certainly dissuaded the British naval commanders from attempting an assault on the port of New York, as they had at Washington and Baltimore. With the conclusion of hostilities in 1814, Ellis Island was almost deserted for over twenty years, save for the occasional crowds which gathered to observe executions.

In the years preceding the Civil War, Fort Gibson was staffed, at various times, by both the Army and the Navy. The Navy Department built a powder magazine on the site in 1835, but in 1841 the Army was given responsibility for the installation. At no time did either service place many men on the island, and in 1861 Appleton's *Cyclopedia* gave the total population of Ellis Island as five.

In 1846, famine in Ireland sent thousands of starving immigrants streaming into New England and New York. Perhaps sensing that the island was hardly being used by the military, the New York State Commissioners of Emigration wrote to the War Department in 1847 requesting permission to use the old fort to house "Convalescent Emigrants." "Ellis Island," Secretary of War Marcy replied, "is very small; it is the site of a naval magazine, containing large supplies of ammunition; the government has not . . . allowed any person other than a proper guard, to reside on the island." The state did not press the issue. After 1861, the naval arsenal was enlarged

Guadalupe women(French West Indies) SS "Korona" Apr

Missionaries
May 1908.

and a few heavy guns were added to the Fort Gibson defenses, but the station served only as a supply station behind the lines throughout the Civil War.

Shortly after the conclusion of the war, the New York *Sun* shocked its readers by claiming that the munitions stockpiled on Ellis Island could explode, and "that New York, Brooklyn, Jersey City, and the numerous villages on Staten Island are now, and have been for a long time, in imminent peril of being at once destroyed by the explosions of the magazines on Ellis Island." *Harper's Weekly,* in an article in 1868, noted that Fort Gibson was packed with 3,000 barrels of gunpowder and "a very large number of shells." *Harper's* questioned the necessity of so large a quantity of explosives "in such close proximity to the most populous city in the country." The Navy made no reply to these charges and *Harper's* and the *Sun* eventually dropped the matter. The danger of a magazine explosion on the island continued to be a matter of concern, however, and in 1876, Congressman Hardenbaugh of New Jersey proposed a resolution in the House that would order the immediate abandonment of Ellis Island as the site of a munitions arsenal. "If it were struck by lightning," he maintained, "the shock would destroy Jersey City, Hoboken, and parts of New York." The congress ignored his fears, and though some people remained uneasy, the powder magazine was left on the island.

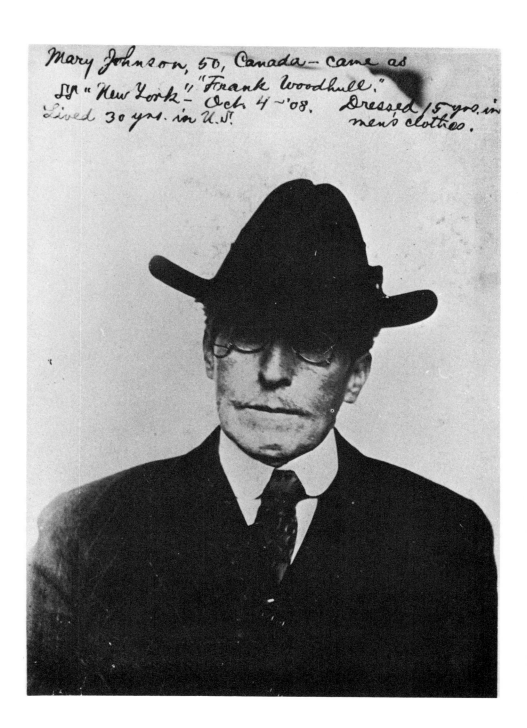

Mary Johnson, 50, Canada — came as SS "New York" "Frank Woodhull." Oct. 4 ~ '08. Dressed 15 yrs. in men's clothes. Lived 30 yrs. in U.S.

English-Jews.

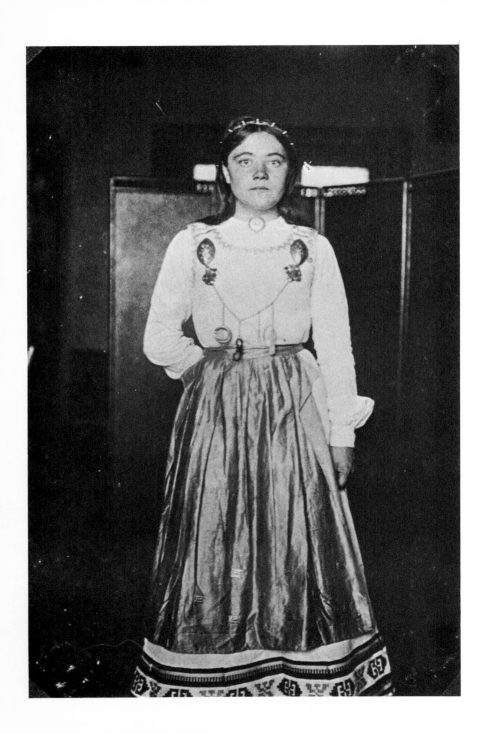

Though its impact was not felt immediately, a bill passed by Congress in 1882 was to have a great effect on the future of Ellis Island. The law excluded from settling in the United States "any convict, lunatic, idiot, or any person unable to take care of himself or herself without becoming a public charge." Prior to this time, the government left to the states the task of determining the desirability of immigrants. Beginning in the 1880's, however, (and continuing well into the twentieth century), recurrent newspaper and magazine stories told of degenerate aliens being cast out of European and Asian alms houses, insane asylums and prisons, and dumped on the shores of America. Once here, the stories went, they almost invariably became public charges. In many respects, this theme was little different from that of the Know-Nothings in the 1850's, and, as in the years following the Great Famine in Ireland, there was a germ of truth buried in these hysterical statements.

While the bulk of the newcomers to America in the nineteenth and early twentieth centuries did not become public charges, there is some evidence that lax or non-existent state immigration laws before 1882 did allow the entry of persons who were almost certain to become public charges. Even in the "First Wave" of immigration (prior to 1890), which was made up largely of people of Northern European stock, there were sufficient numbers of very poor families to strain the resources of the public charity funds of many municipalities. Certainly some of the immigrants, living in wretched poverty, were tempted to achieve upward mobility through one of the few careers open to them—crime. And in many cities, immigrants did constitute a disproportionate percentage of both public charity rolls and prison populations.

Immigrant from Ruthenia

To the workingman, the immigrant seemed to pose a real threat. In an era when job security was all but nonexistent, alien laborers willing to work for subsistence wages were met with hostility by native workers. Led by Terrence Powderly, the Knights of Labor and other early unions agitated for the restriction of immigration. They argued that the importation of skilled European artisans to compete with Americans would impoverish all native workers. In 1885, the Alien Contract Labor Law made it illegal to bring foreigners to the United States for labor under contract. The passage of the Contract Labor and Immigration laws made it necessary to set up a much more thorough screening process for immigrants, but for a number of years little new administrative machinery was initiated for their enforcement. The Federal government contracted with state commissions of immigration for the execution of the laws, and a head tax of fifty cents (later raised to four dollars) was placed on immigrants to help pay the cost of cursory examinations.

In New York, where the majority of immigrants arrived, the federal-state system of administration was racked by jurisdictional disputes, incompetence and corruption. A House committee investigating charges of mismanagement reported that the existing facilities on the Battery made it "almost impossible to properly inspect the large numbers of persons who arrive daily," and one of the New York State Commissioners described the administration as "a perfect farce." The Treasury Department, which was the administrative agency charged with executing the new immigration laws, determined that the processing of newcomers would have to

be handled exclusively by the federal government. Congress appointed a joint committee to recommend a location for an immigration station.

A member of the committee, Senator McPherson of New Jersey, suggested that the dangerous munitions dump on Ellis Island be dismantled, and the island converted into an immigration center. Secretary of the Treasury Windon had visited Ellis Island and concluded that "it was not a desirable place; and we were so advised by the Collector of Customs at New York and some others who were with us." Nevertheless, the Congressional group chose this location, and $150,000 was appropriated in May, 1890, to begin construction of the depot.

The selection of Ellis Island had several advantages. The government already owned the property, the island was nearly uninhabited, and using it as an immigration center would allay the fears of those people who were still uneasy about having a magazine so close to a heavily populated area. One historian of Ellis Island, Willard Heaps, has noted that "on an island immigrants could be both protected and guided," and not immediately subjected to the confusion and exploitation of the city. It should also be pointed out that the location of the Immigration Station of the Port of New York on an island perfectly fulfilled the intention of the immigration laws by making it extremely difficult for "undesirables" to escape and mingle with the crowds of the city. The only other site given serious consideration was Bedloe's Island, the location of the Statue of Liberty. Objections to placing the station there were led by the New York *World* which claimed that what was to be a park would now "be converted into a Babel,"

and the proposal was dropped. Whatever the reasons for selecting Ellis Island, the building of the immigration center was an expensive and difficult undertaking.

During 1891, hundreds of workmen labored at a large, three story reception center, a hospital for ill or quarantined immigrants, a laundry, boilerhouse and electric generating plant; most of these buildings were constructed of Georgia pine. The powder magazine was removed, and with the completion of sea walls, landfill almost doubled the size of the island. In addition, it was necessary to dredge a channel to the shallow island some 200 feet wide and 1,200 feet long. The cost of this very large construction effort amounted to well over half a million dollars. When completed, Ellis Island was a self-contained city whose population, while transient, could often be numbered in the thousands.

While the facilities were being erected, Congress expanded the scope of the law of 1882. It excluded aliens who were polygamists, and those "suffering from a loathesome or dangerous contagious disease." Aliens who became public charges due to disabilities they brought with them, but which had escaped notice upon entry, could be deported within one year. Steamship companies were obliged to exercise greater care in selling passage to would-be immigrants because the government required them to return to their homeland, free of charge, all immigrants rejected by the authorities, and to pay for the meals of any aliens detained for further examination on the island.

The Ellis Island Immigration Station was officially dedicated on New Year's Day, 1892. *Harper's Weekly* was enthusiastic in its description of the facilities:

June 4th — 1897.

It looks like a latter-day watering place hotel, presenting to the view a great many-windowed expanse of buff-painted wooden walls, of blue slate roofing and of light and picturesque towers . . . It is devised to permit the handling of at least 10,000 immigrants in a day, and the first story, which is 13 feet in height, is sufficiently capacious for the storage and handling of the baggage of 12,000 newcomers.

Five years later, the Commissioner of Immigration, Dr. Joseph Senner, was to describe the structures as "a row of unsightly, ramshackle tinderboxes," but on that cold, first day of 1892, the buildings must have looked most impressive to the immigration officials who had been confined to cramped quarters on Manhattan's Battery. The first passenger to land was a Miss Annie Moore, aged fifteen, of County Cork, Ireland. Doubtless she was confused by the clanging of bells and shrieking of whistles which celebrated the opening of the station. After successfully answering the questions of the immigration officials, she was presented with a ten-dollar gold piece, to commemorate the occasion. In its first day of operation, seven hundred immigrants followed Annie through the station, and in the rest of the year, just under 450,000 newcomers passed through the great reception hall. The immigration inspectors were kept busy, but beginning in 1893 a severe depression greatly reduced the number of foreigners entering the country throughout the rest of the decade.

In the early morning of June 14, 1897, a fire of undetermined origin completely destroyed the wooden structures on Ellis Island. The immigrants who were sleeping in the station's hospital and dormitories were quickly rounded up and evacuated to New York. Perhaps the greatest loss suffered in the blaze was the destruction of almost all the immigration records for the port of New York for the years from 1855 to 1890. "Fear of something like this fire has haunted me," Commissioner Senner stated, " . . . and when the Government rebuilds it will be forced to put up decent fireproof structures." Congress appropriated $600,000 to rebuild the Ellis Island station, and the work began almost immediately.

As the construction progressed on the new facilities, immigrants were received in several Treasury Department buildings at the tip of Manhattan. The steamer *Narragansett* was leased and fitted out as a detention center for questionable aliens; it was docked at Ellis Island and detainees were transferred to it for overnight accommodations. The temporary quarters of the immigration station could hardly have been better designed to produce chaos, and in this they succeeded admirably. On many days over a thousand confused immigrants milled about as harried officials and guards shouted the requisite questions in order to be heard over the din.

Finally, in December of 1900, the new buildings on Ellis Island were occupied. The immigration officers almost certainly set foot in the new reception hall with a sigh of relief. For thirty months they had processed an average of more than 20,000 aliens per month in facilities designed to handle barely half that number. The large brick and iron structures included a reception and inspection center which was 338 feet long and 168 feet wide, and on each corner of the building turrets rose to a height of 100 feet. On the first floor there was sufficient space for the baggage of new arrivals. A wide staircase led to the Registry Room on the second floor where

Main building after fire

the immigrant was examined; this hall, with ceilings almost 60 feet high, was bright and airy, and seemed more than sufficient to accommodate a great number of immigrants on any given day.

The building of the New Immigration Station on Ellis Island had cost the government over one million dollars, but with the end of the depression of the 1890's, greater numbers of immigrants were expected to arrive in the port of New York. The substantial Victorian buildings were fireproof and had a look of permanence and solidarity. The investment of considerable effort and expense in building the new facilities demonstrated that the government, despite some exclusionary measures, fully expected to process immigrants for decades to come.

Although the new immigration center was well designed to handle the rush of southern and eastern Europeans which had just begun, the administration of the station was often lax and corrupt. Jobs on Ellis Island were subject to a high degree of patronage on both the federal and state level, and lucrative contracts were passed out to the party faithful for services and supplies necessary to the operation of Ellis Island. Worst of all, the temptation to take advantage of the confused and frightened foreigners who flooded into the port clutching their life savings proved to be too great for many of the administrators and workers on Ellis Island.

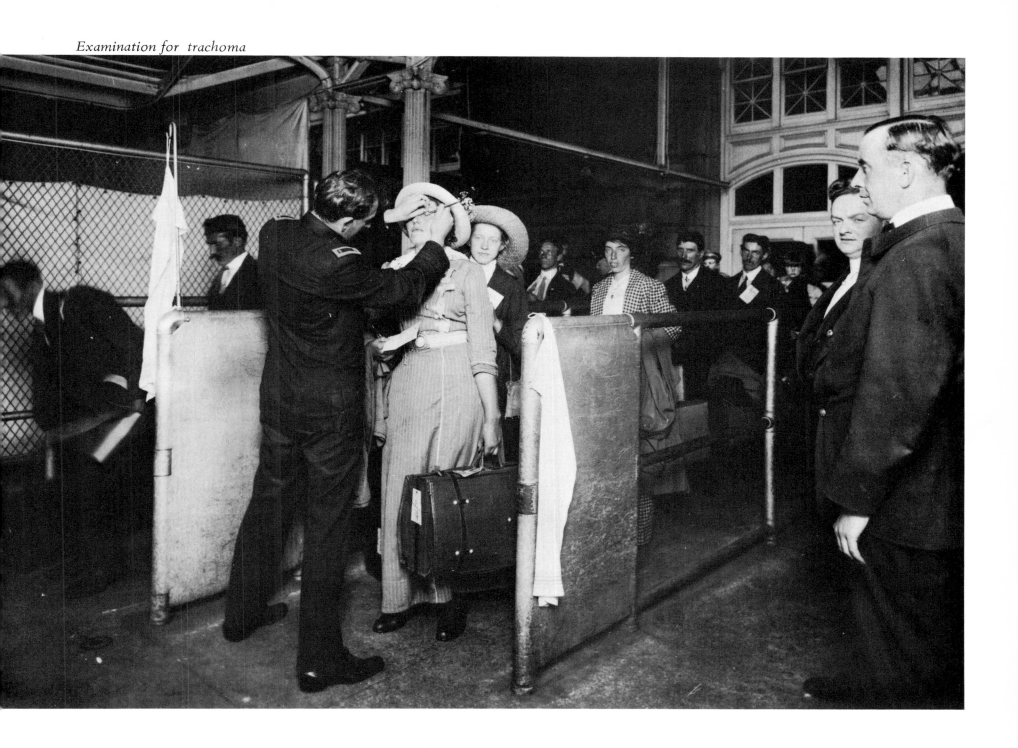

Examination for trachoma

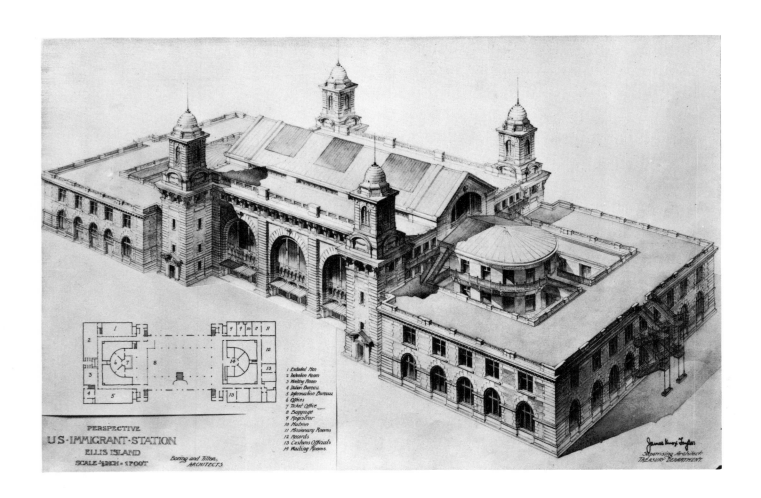

PERSPECTIVE
U·S·IMMIGRANT·STATION
ELLIS ISLAND
SCALE ½ INCH = 1 FOOT

Boring and Tilton,
ARCHITECTS

1 Excluded Men
2 Detention Room
3 Waiting Room
4 Union Bureau
5 Information Bureau
6 Offices
7 Ticket Office
8 Baggage
9 Registry
10 Matron
11 Missionary Rooms
12 Records
13 Customs Officials
14 Waiting Rooms

James Knox Taylor
Supervising Architect
TREASURY DEPARTMENT

Immigrants waiting to be transferred

John D. Third and family, natives of Scotland,
ex SS "Caledonia", September 17, 1905. Went to
friend, John Fleming, Anniston, Alabama.

"The management of the Ellis Island business," President Theodore Roosevelt was to observe, "has been rotten . . ." Scandals of robbery and extortion were common in the first years of the new Ellis Island Station. In 1901, Commissioner of Immigration Fitchie requested an increase in the number of policemen to protect aliens from robbery and fraud. Charges were common that immigrants were short-changed at the money conversion concession, and over-charged in the restaurant and railroad ticket offices, and in search for a new Commissioner of Immigration, Roosevelt remarked, "I am more anxious to get this office straight than almost any other." There was some evidence that immigrants who were initially rejected for medical or other reasons could buy their way into America. Conversely, those who arrived on Ellis Island possessing substantial sums of money were often detained for "questioning." "The resulting power of blackmail," wrote Roosevelt's new Commissioner, William Williams, "will readily be seen."

In his attempt to reorganize Ellis Island, President Roosevelt ran into substantial political resistance but the conditions which Williams uncovered hardened T.R.'s resolve to "make a thorough sweeping out" of the management of the station. The New Commissioner took office in 1902, and in his first report stated that under earlier administrations, immigrants were often treated in a manner "not calculated to make upon them a favorable impression at the time of their first contact with the institutions of this country." Williams was most shocked by the highly unsanitary conditions in the station. The dining room floor "was allowed by the former privilege holder (Commissioner) to remain covered with grease, bones, and other remnants

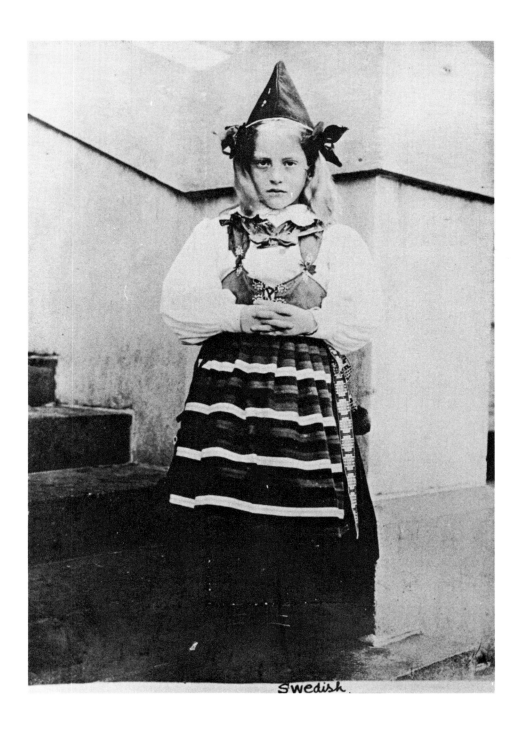

Swedish.

of food for days at a time." He reported that the dishes used by the immigrants were used repeatedly without washing. With the backing of the President, Williams launched a campaign to clean up both the facilities and personnel on the island. By removing corrupt officials and concessionaires, reforming the inspection routine, and improving the sanitation conditions, the Williams administration improved to some degree the reputation of Ellis Island which had won it the sobriquet, "The Isle of Tears."

Even with an honest administration in charge of Ellis Island, newcomers were sometimes paralyzed with fear when questioned by immigration officials. In the villages of Italy, Russia, Greece and elsewhere, stories were circulated about people who were rejected at Ellis Island for looking "suspicious" or for failing to answer promptly the questions put to them.

Although the great majority of the immigrants were admitted to the United States, the consequences of deportation for those who were denied entry could be severe. The average European peasant generally had to sell all his possessions and property and sometimes go into debt to finance the passage to America. Deportation for such people could mean complete impoverishment; but for the Jew fleeing Czarist pogroms, the possibility of forcible return to Russia could quite literally be a matter of life and death. Some individuals could not face the disgrace and ruin of deportation, and there were three thousand suicides on Ellis Island during its 40 years of operation as a processing center. For the person emigrating from his native country, the rewards for settling in America seemed great, but the risks could be enormous.

And yet they came by the millions. In one of the greatest migrations in human history,

Roumanian.

Europeans deserted their homes and packed themselves into the holds of ships for the journey across the Atlantic. From 1890 to 1930, almost 16,000,000 immigrants entered America through the port of New York. The scale of this human flood is staggering. In those few decades, immigrants passed through the port of New York in sufficient numbers to populate the present cities of Los Angeles, Baltimore, Atlanta, Dallas, New Orleans, St. Louis, Cleveland, San Francisco, Philadelphia, Chicago, and Boston!

For the average European the first step in a journey to America was making the eventful decision to leave his home. Very often, one member of the family would set out for the United States and, if he prospered, would pay the way for other members of his family. First would come the father, then the mother and children, and in time, grandparents, uncles, cousins and in-laws would follow.

From his town or village the prospective American would go to the nearest port of embarkation. A steerage ticket usually cost about $35. After a quick medical examination, vaccination, and the filing of a lengthy questionnaire with the shipping company, the immigrant got a visa from the United States consul and, if required, from his own country, then boarded his ship shortly before it cast off.

Steerage: the word evokes images of cramped quarters, wretched conditions, suffering and pain. And at its best, steerage was extremely uncomfortable. The experiences of a woman investigator who disguised herself as a Bohemian peasant and made the crossing in steerage are illuminating:

All the steerage berths were of iron, the framework forming two tiers and having but a low

Antonio Pestincola – 37.
Italian Piper
S.S. "San Giovanni"
May 12 – '08.

partition between the individual berths. Each bunk contained a mattress filled with straw . . . there were no pillows. A short and light-weight white blanket was the only covering provided . . .

The floors in all these compartments were of wood. They were swept every morning and the aisles sprinkled with sand. None of them was washed during the twelve days' voyage nor was there any indication that a disinfectant was being used on them. The beds received only such attention as each occupant gave to his own.

Two washrooms were provided for the use of the steerage. The first morning out I took special care to inquire for the women's wash room. One of the crew directed me to a door bearing the sign Washroom for Men. Within were both men and women. Thinking I had been misdirected, I proceeded to the other washroom. This bore no label and was likewise being used by both sexes . . . The small basins served as a dishpan for washing greasy tins, as a laundry tub for soiled handkerchiefs and clothing, and as a basin for shampoos, and without receiving any special cleaning. It was the only receptacle to be found for use in the case of seasickness . . . Steerage passengers may be filthy, as is often alleged, but considering the total absence of conveniences for keeping clean, this uncleanliness seems but a natural consequence.

During these twelve days in the steerage I lived in a disorder and in surroundings that offended every sense. Only the fresh breeze from the sea overcame the sickening odors . . . Everything was dirty, sticky, and disagreeable to the touch. Every impression was offensive.

14

A steerage voyage could condemn a passenger to ten to fifteen days of total misery. At its worst, people were crowded into small spaces with little ventilation, and meager facilities for personal cleanliness. On a rough passage, the roar of the engines just below him, the stale air, the smell of vomit on the decks and the rolling of the ship doubtless convinced many a traveller that he had made a terrible mistake.

Whatever the conditions on individual vessels, the steerage passengers provided a bonanza for the shipping companies. Large liners held between 1,500 and 2,000 passengers in steerage, and companies could realize ticket sales of $50,000 or more for the trip across the Atlantic. As historian Willard Heaps has pointed out: "Companies were able to meet the basic costs of the voyage from the much higher revenues of the two cabin classes, leaving the income from steerage as clear profit. The cost of steerage food was kept minimal: the largest liners could feed one immigrant for sixty cents per day."

Johanna Dijkhoff, 40 - Holland - with 11 chev. "Noordam" May 12 '08. to Loretta, Minn.

Guadalupe women (French West Indies)
SS "Korona", April 6, 1911.

15

Not all the immigrants arriving in New York came in the steerage quarters. Well-to-do aliens travelled in the comparative comfort of cabin or first class. Foreigners who arrived in these more expensive sections of the ship were processed by immigration authorities who came on board soon after the vessel entered New York harbor. This examination was usually cursory, and except for those who seemed suspicious, "the better sort" of immigrant was allowed to land in New York and thus avoid Ellis Island altogether.

This practice was, of course, thoroughly undemocratic, but it occasionally worked to the immigrant's benefit. Families travelling in steerage would sometimes purchase a cabin or even first class ticket for an aged parent or sickly child and avoid a more thorough examination on Ellis Island. If a passenger was obviously suffering from physical or mental illness, the inspectors would usually insist on an examination by the physicians on Ellis Island. But in marginal cases, families were often kept together by this trick.

While the cabin class passengers were being inspected, the immigrants in steerage usually began to gather up their baggage and crowded onto the deck in hopes of seeing their new country. After the inspectors left in their cutter, the ship would steam through the Narrows between Staten Island and Brooklyn and into Upper New York Bay.

Immigrant from Sweden

16

The emotions of the passengers—anticipation, excitement, fear—were soon overcome by surprise and awe. Close to Ellis Island was the massive Statue of Liberty, whose symbolism was not lost on these newcomers. As the ship moved closer to the immigration station, the skyline of lower Manhattan came into view. And what a sight it was!

Many of the immigrants had never seen a building of more than two or three stories, but by the turn of the century, 20 and 30-story buildings were clustered in solid masses around the financial district and along Broadway. By 1908, the 47-story Singer Building had added its profile to the skyline, and in 1913, the enormous 60-floor Woolworth Building was completed. Most of the immigrants had heard stories of the magic towers of New York, but the sight of the real thing was impressive and overwhelming. Sometimes cheering, singing and dancing would erupt on the steerage decks as the ship moved into the harbor. More often a profound silence interrupted only by the crying of babies would descend on the crowd.

As the immigrants in steerage stared at their destination, the first and cabin class foreigners and United States citizens were dropped off at a New York or Hoboken pier, and then the steerage passengers were led to a dock where barges took them to Ellis Island. Though relieved that the voyage was over, most of the immigrants knew that the most important test was yet to come.

On many occasions during the peak years of immigration, from 1903 to 1914, several large ships would enter New York harbor on the same day, and the immigrants were then required to wait at the pier for several hours before boarding one of the barges. While waiting, the nervous aliens were often approached by dishonest peddlers. Broughton Brandenburg, a reporter who made several trips in steerage disguised as an immigrant, wrote in 1904:

While we were waiting . . . we had time to buy something to eat from the fruit and cake vendors. Though it was mid-October, five cents was asked for apples to be had on any street corner in New York for one cent, and ten cents for a slice of thick yellow cake that was the worst mess of coloring matter, adulterated flour and soda, I have ever set my teeth into. It was heavy like stone and was gritty . . . On top of all this, when we paid for it in silver Italian money, the vendors allowed only seventeen cents for a lire, when taking them at nineteen cents would have been a profit.

Eleazar Kaminietzky – 26 – Russ. Hebrew
SS "Hamburg" June 25 – 1914. Vegetarian

18

Steerage passengers were assigned to groups of thirty people, and tags with their names and identification numbers were pinned to their clothing. Groupings of thirty people came about because thirty was the maximum number of names that would fit on each passenger manifest sheet. These sheets were filled out at the port of embarkation and listed most of the vital statistics the immigration authorities required. A tag marked "A-25" meant that the person was the twenty-fifth name on sheet "A".

Filing off the barges at Ellis Island, the immigrants were met by an interpreter and led to the reception building. They were directed to climb the stairs on the east side of the hall. There they encountered several teams of medical examiners, who looked for any obvious mental or physical defects. The scalp and throat were checked, as were the hands and neck. The doctors were well acquainted with the symptoms of most contagious diseases, and a rapid examination was usually enough to spot infected individuals. The inspectors also watched to see if immigrants who had just carried their baggage up the stairs seemed unusually weak or winded, or gave evidence of a limp.

After passing the first team of doctors, the newcomer moved to another medical inspector who checked his eyes. Then, if he passed this test, he was led to a small enclosure where he and the rest of his group waited for an interpreter to direct them to the registry section. Those who did not pass the medical examination had their clothing marked with a piece of chalk and were directed to a detention area for closer examination.

While waiting on the hard wooden benches for the long-feared cross-examination of the registration officer, many immigrants doubtless repeated, again and again, the responses they would give to the expected questions. This questioning was almost invariably not as dreadful as they had imagined. The inspector was primarily interested in making sure that statements on the ship's manifest were correct, and in weeding out contract laborers. Still, a small percentage was detained and ultimately deported, and wild rumors of trick questions and impossible demands kept entire shiploads of passengers rehearsing the "right" answers for their entire voyage across the Atlantic.

"Your name?" "How did you pay your passage?" ("My own money.") "Has a job been promised to you?" ("No!") "Are you an anarchist?" ("No!!") "Are you going to join a relative or a friend? If so, what is his name and address?" And so on. Each immigrant was asked about twenty questions. Interpreters were always on hand to translate the questions and answers. Many immigrants fingered sums of money which they thought would be necessary to buy the approval of the examiner. They were asked how much money they had brought with them not because there was any specific sum necessary for entry, but to keep a check on the currency concession which changed marks, rubles, lire and many other currencies into dollars.

Roumanians.

Immigrants who aroused the suspicion of the inspector were indicated by a coded chalk mark and detained. Stories of impoverished immigrant girls becoming "fallen women," or being lured into America by rings of international white-slavers, were common in the first decades of the twentieth century. An unescorted woman was usually questioned by a matron who tried to determine her "moral character," and almost invariably she was detained on the island until a relative or respectable friend came for her. Every immigrant who was detained was brought before a three-man board of inquiry and questioned. If the board recommended deportation, the alien could appeal to the Ellis Island Commissioner and the Commissioner of Immigration in Washington.

The great majority of those who entered the reception area (between 90 and 95 percent) were marked in the ledger as "approved for entry" and handed a card bearing the single word "Admitted." The actual inspection process took 45 minutes or less except when large crowds of immigrants strained the capacity of the center and made long waits necessary. When the inspectors were unable to examine all those who arrived on a given day, the immigrants were kept overnight on the island and their meals paid for by the steamship companies which had brought them.

Aretz   Carballo   Knauer   Doering.

Russian giant

Those who held the precious "Admitted" tickets were directed to the currency exchange and to the area where railroad tickets could be purchased. More than two-thirds of the immigrants were bound for destinations other than New York and the railroad ticket offices often did more than $40,000 in business in a single day. For those who were going to New York City, relatives were usually waiting in a room nearby, and noisy, emotional scenes were common. On rare occasions, however, these meetings were not altogether pleasant. Some women came to America to marry men they had never seen, and when their proposed spouses came to fetch them, refused to leave with them and begged to be deported. Other matches arranged by European marriage brokers never were completed because of unplanned shipboard romances, and hundreds of marriages were performed on Ellis Island.

On any given day, at least a few people were detained on Ellis Island, not for medical or legal reasons, but simply because they were unable to communicate to the translators, railroad officials, or examiners where they wanted to go. After much head-scratching, someone would usually figure out that the man whose destination was "Pringvilliamas" was bound for Springfield, Mass.; and immigration officers became quite adept at deciphering such words as "Linkinbra" or "Pillsburs" as Lincoln, Nebraska, and Pittsburgh.

UNRESTRICTED IMMIGRATION AND ITS RESULTS.—A POSSIBLE CURIOSITY OF THE TWENTIETH CENTURY. THE LAST YANKEE.

SEE PAGE 50.

Hungarian

Jakob Mithelstadt and family, Russian Germans, ex SS "Pretoria", May 9, 1905. Admitted to go to Kuln, N. D.

Slavian Gipsies.

23

In the early morning hours of July 30, 1916, the war came to Ellis Island. Located only a few hundred yards from the immigration center were a railroad yard and barge loading facility just off the Jersey coast, known as Black Tom Island. Loaded on at least fourteen barges and railroad cars were tons of munitions destined for Russia. On the evening of the 30th, German saboteurs set off an explosion of such force that windows were broken in midtown Manhattan and shocks were felt as far as Philadelphia.

Sleeping on Ellis Island that night were 625 detainees and employees. The initial blast blew out all the windows and many of the doors, but the solid brick structures did not collapse. The island's staff immediately herded the panic-stricken immigrants to the relative shelter of the eastern side of the island and placed them on barges. They were taken to Manhattan while shells, bullets, and rockets exploded around them. By sunrise of the next day, the Ellis Island facilities had suffered nearly $400,000 in damage, but, surprisingly, there had been no deaths or even major injuries. Repairs were begun immediately.

24

In the Spring of 1917, the United States entered the war, and the crews of Central Power ships in the harbor were arrested and sent to Ellis Island for internment. The 1,500 German sailors on the island were soon joined by over 2,000 "suspicious" people of German origin who were locked up there. After a few months, these prisoners were moved to camps in the South, and the War Department took over the management of the station for the duration of the "War to End All Wars". The few immigrants who dared to cross the Atlantic in wartime were processed as usual, but the Ellis Island hospitals were filled with sick and wounded soldiers, and the dormitories were often crowded with sailors awaiting assignment.

25

An even more atypical group lived on Ellis Island after the close of the war. In response to the Russian Revolution, Congress passed an Act in 1918 which called for the "exclusion and expulsion of all United States aliens who are members of the anarchistic and similar classes." Beginning in the fall of 1919, the infamous "Red Scare" seized the nation, and Attorney General A. Mitchell Palmer led a series of raids which netted thousands of labor agitators, "Bolsheviks," and anarchists. By June of 1920, several thousand radicals had been arrested and were being held for questioning and, ultimately, deportation. Several shiploads of supposed subversives were sent to Russia, the most famous being the *Budford* (popularly known as the "Red Ark") among whose passengers were Emma Goldman and Alexander Berkman. By mid-1920, however, the hysteria had spent itself and Ellis Island was prepared for an expected deluge of immigrants fleeing the shattered countries of Europe.

Immigrant from Rumania

Swedish girls.

The influx of millions of new inhabitants in a comparatively short time was bound to bring about a reaction. From the 1890's until the outbreak of World War I, an increasing percentage of immigrants arriving in America was from southern and eastern Europe. Americans had had a difficult enough time assimilating earlier waves of Germans, Scandinavians, and Irish, but the "New Immigration" composed of Italians, Slavs and Jews seemed extremely unlikely candidates for "Americanization."

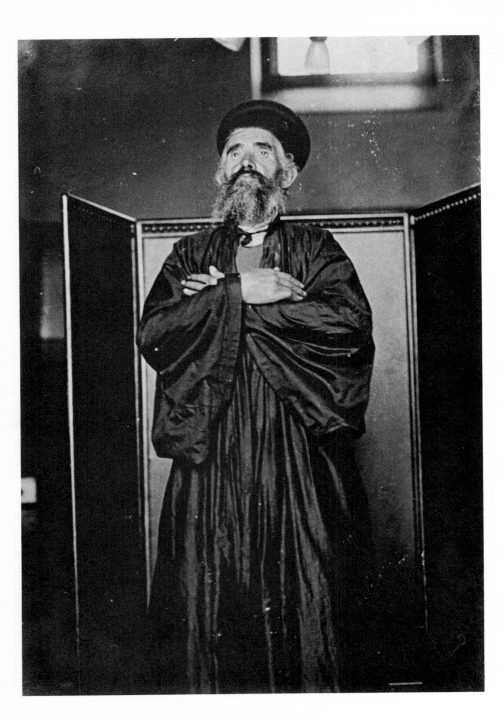

As the immigrant ghettos like New York's Lower East Side grew in size, a number of voices, some rational and others tinged with acute paranoia, were raised in protest. In one of the most popular books of the second decade of the twentieth century *(The Passing of a Great Race,* 1916) Madison Grant, an American anthropologist wrote of "the racial nondescripts who are now flocking here":

These new immigrants were no longer exclusively members of the Nordic race as were the earlier ones who came of their own impulse to improve their social conditions. The transportation lines advertised America as a land flowing with milk and honey and the European governments took the opportunity to unload upon careless, wealthy and hospitable America the sweepings of their jails and asylums . . . The new immigration . . . contained a large and increasing number of the weak, the broken and the mentally crippled of all races drawn from the lowest stratum of the Mediterranean basin and the Balkans, together with hoards of the wretched, submerged populations of the Polish ghettos. Our jails, insane asylums, and alms-houses are filled with this human flotsam . . .

These immigrants adopt the language of the native American, they wear his clothes, they steal his name and they are beginning to take his women, but they seldom adopt his religion or understand his ideals, and while he is being elbowed out of his own home the American looks calmly abroad and urges on others the suicidal ethics which are exterminating his own race.

Main Hall

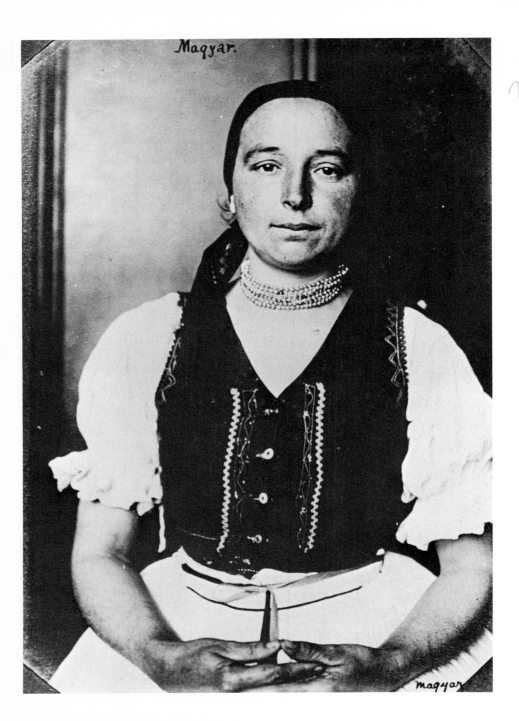

Extreme arguments for restriction such as Grant's were not uncommon, and a great many long-time Americans sincerely feared the impact of the immigrant on local and national political life. The foreigners, they agreed, seemed to flock to the support of corrupt urban bosses, and some were certainly infected with alien political notions—anarchism, syndicalism, Bolshevism. An article in *The Popular Science Monthly* in 1913 argued that: "Restriction is necessary if our truly American ideals and institutions are to persist, and if our inherited stock of good American manhood is not to be depreciated." Added to the fears for political institutions was the seeming menace to public health brought about by the supposedly filthy habits of the new immigrants. Magazine articles describing the dangers of alien infection and the spread of contagious diseases were common throughout the period from 1890 to 1918. "Why," asked a writer in a 1914 issue of *Survey* magazine, "should we get this mass of diseases from immigrants arriving by sea?" Public demands that immigration be curtailed or eliminated altogether produced a great deal of sentiment in Congress for restrictive legislation. In 1917, Congress overrode President Wilson's veto and required all adult immigrants entering the United States to be able to read at least thirty words of English or their own native language. Similar bills had been vetoed by Presidents Cleveland and Taft, but Wilson's objection was that the literacy test was "not a test of character, or quality, or of personal fitness" was ignored.

The literacy test was sometimes difficult to enforce, and in 1920, there seemed to be millions of sufficiently literate Europeans ready to come to the New World. "Ever since 1914," observed the *New York Times* somewhat petulantly, "it has been obvious that the end of the war would bring a tide of immigrants, yet not one effective step has been taken to cope with it."

In 1920, a new wave of immigrants seemed destined to reach pre-war levels, and public demands for restriction became insistent. On May 19, 1921, Congress passed a bill which limited the number of immigrants entering the United States to 357,000 per year. The quota law limited immigration to three percent of the number of each nationality residing in the United States in 1910. The measure had the effect of severely reducing immigration from southern and eastern Europe and encouraging an actual increase in the number of arrivals from northern and western Europe. No more than 20 percent of a country's quota was allowed to enter in any one month. The statute was to take effect in fifteen days.

The impact of this new law was immediately felt on Ellis Island. Edward Corsi, an immigrant himself who served as Commissioner on Ellis Island during the 1930's and who was one of the first historians of the island, has written: "The final week before the law became effective saw a mad dash of thousands to American shores. Imagine the ships, bulging with human cargo, racing through the Narrows and into New York harbor, actually colliding with one another in their hurry to be at Ellis Island before the last minute of grace." Steamship companies feared the loss of highly profitable steerage revenue and would race to unload their passengers in the first days of each month. It was sometimes necessary to admit thousands of immigrants on "parole" who were unknowingly brought to America after their national quota was exhausted. A physician on Ellis Island recalled a scene which took place soon after the passage of the Quota Law:

A (great) . . . tragedy was a shipload of 500 immigrants from southeastern Europe who had disposed of their homes and all their possessions to start life anew on American shores, only to find that they were forced to return. The ensuing demonstration of these excitable people is one of my most painful reminiscences of service at the island. They screamed and bawled and beat about like wild animals, breaking the waiting-room furniture and attacking the attendants, several of whom were severely hurt. It was a pitiful spectacle . . .

Subsequent immigration laws further restricted the flow of Europeans to America. In 1924, an act set the quota for each nationality at "two percent of the number of foreign-born individuals of such nationality resident in the United States as determined by the census of 1890." Immigrants from southern and eastern Europe were almost completely barred from entry since very few had settled in the United States prior to 1890. Italy, for example, was allowed only 3,845 immigrants a year under the new quota system. The great migration had come to an end.

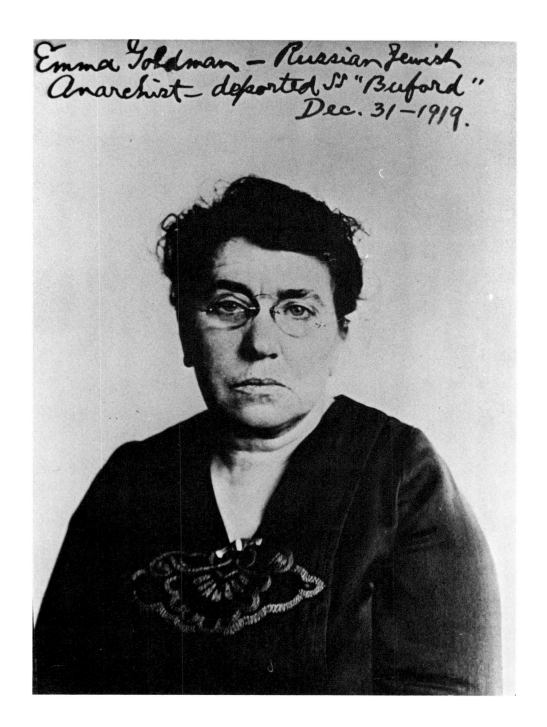

Emma Goldman — Russian Jewish Anarchist — deported SS "Buford" Dec. 31—1919.

Helen R. Bastido and Orman Louis

Belgian
Stowaway
vs "U.S.a.T.
Cantigny"—
Admitted on
Bond
Feb. 22
1921.

Throughout the 1930's, Ellis Island processed a comparative trickle of immigrants and refugees from Hitler's Germany. When America entered the Second World War, the island was once again used for detention of enemy aliens and suspected Axis spies. By the end of the war almost all processing of immigrants was handled by American consulates, and Ellis Island was maintained largely as a housing facility for aliens awaiting deportation.

With the passage of the Internal Security Act of 1950, the population of the island soon rose to almost 1500 people. The act provided for the exclusion and deportation of subversive aliens. All immigrants arriving in New York were cross-examined, and any who seemed at all suspect were held on the island. The size of this new group placed great stresses on the station's facilities, which had been neglected for almost two decades. It was necessary to open a school on the island for the children of those detained, and for a while, classes for about 125 pupils were held there daily. Some of the detainees were deported and many were held until their political past was investigated, and then released.

In 1954, the government ruled that "only those aliens likely to abscond and those whose release would be inimical to the national security" were to be held in custody for deportation. Deported immigrants were allowed to proceed to their destination under 'parole', and by mid-1954 only about two dozen aliens were still being held. Ellis Island had outlived its usefulness as a deportation center just as it had as an immigration station. In November, 1954, the last immigration officials left the island, and on March 4, 1955, the government declared it to be a "surplus property."

Syrian

What is the value of a national landmark? For several years the government tried to answer this difficult question by soliciting bids from private individuals and corporations. Several members of Congress protested to President Eisenhower that putting a "For Sale" sign on Ellis Island "would be cheap and tawdry." But in 1957 in advertisements in major newspapers across the country, the government announced "that it is now authorized to offer one of the most famous landmarks in the world: ELLIS ISLAND." The site was described as a "perfect location . . . for an oil storage depot, import and export processing, warehousing, manufacturing, private institutions, etc."

Disposing of Ellis Island gave the government more difficulty than acquiring it in the first place. Bids were opened in February, 1958, but all were rejected as too low for the property, and several other auctions were held in 1959 and 1960. There was talk of the government's giving the island to the City of New York for some form of public use, but the city, after examining the property and the deteriorating condition of the buildings, decided that restoring the island would be much too expensive. There were several plans to build a resort on the island, and one builder bid $1,025,000 for the property, but the government rejected this offer. Indeed, there are indications that the government was unsure what to do with Ellis Island. On the one hand, it was insistent that it wanted to sell the property for a high price, but it recognized how embarrassing it would be to sell a piece of the national heritage for whatever price and have it turned into an oil storage depot.

While the discussions about the ultimate fate of Ellis Island were progressing, the buildings of the immigration center were literally falling apart. The grounds were choked with weeds and refuse; the reception center and hospital buildings deteriorated with each passing year. Almost no money was spent on upkeep for the deserted structures, and the combination of weather and neglect took a heavy toll.

From time to time ideas for the use of the island were forwarded to Washington or suggested in the press. These proposals included remaking the station into a women's prison, a drug addiction treatment center, a college, a home for the aged, a school for international affairs, a park, a national center for legalized gambling. In 1962, a New York company bid $2,100,000 for the island. Their plan was to build a self-contained city housing about 8,000 people. In the last month of his life, Frank Lloyd Wright began sketches for the apartment towers, shops and public buildings for the island-city, and the builders hoped to use his plans for the project. But the government rejected this proposal and began to think of converting Ellis Island into a national park and immigration museum.

Intelligence Test

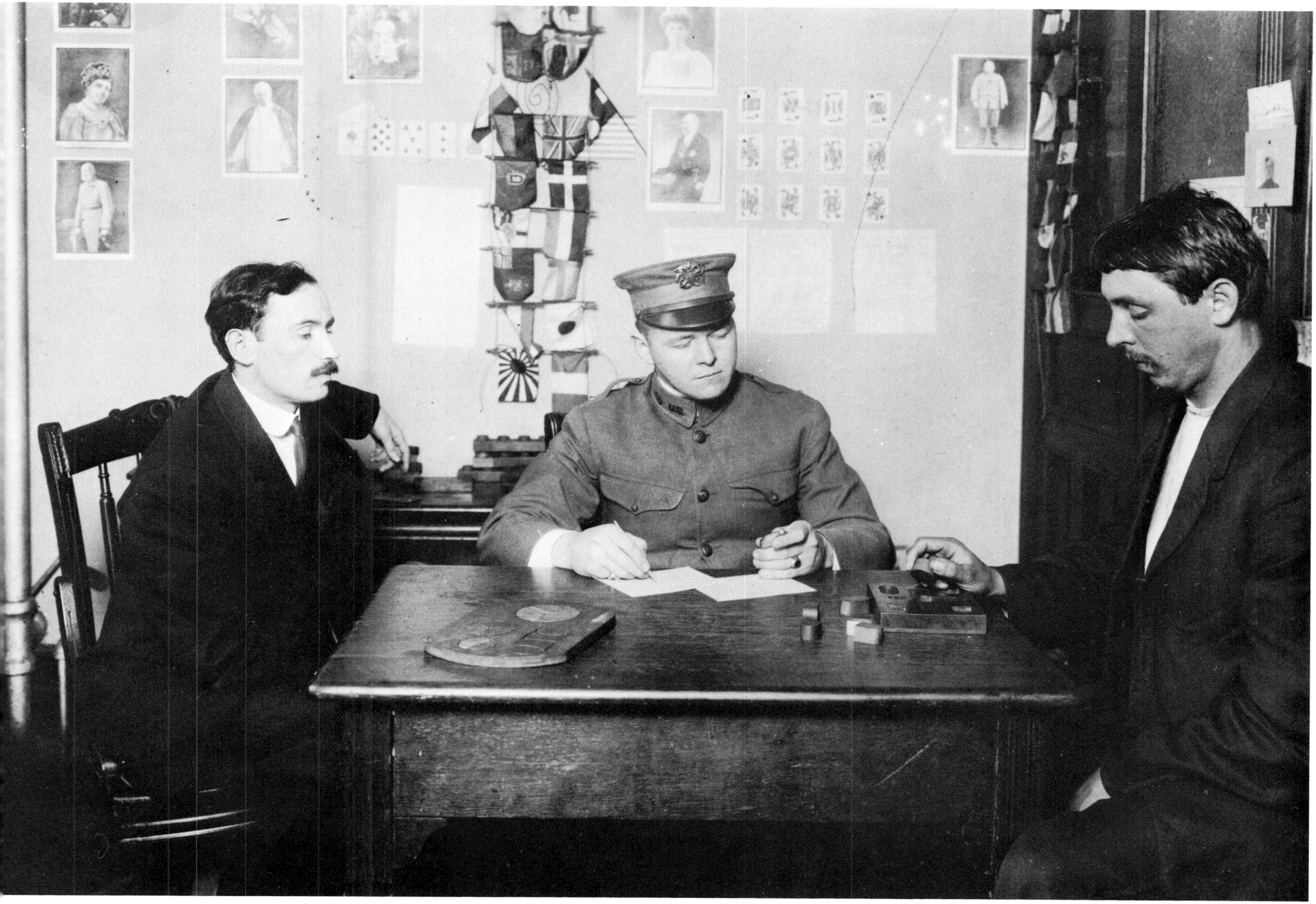

Greek Soldier- Oct-1911.

Secretary of the Interior Stewart Udall suggested in 1964 that the island be added to the Liberty Island National Monument and administered by the National Park Service. In May of 1965, President Lyndon Johnson ordered that the island be officially declared a National Monument. Congress appropriated six million dollars for the construction of an immigration memorial on the island and the planning of a park on the Jersey shore opposite it. Philip Johnson was commissioned to design the memorial and he proposed building a hollow tower 130 feet high. The interior of this structure was to be covered with tiny plaques bearing the names of millions of immigrants who passed through Ellis Island so that, as the visitor ascended to the top, he could try to find the names of relatives or friends. Johnson also made plans to level all the buildings of the immigration station except for the reception hall and a hospital building. These remaining structures were to be partially demolished and vines or ivy trained to grow over the remaining brickwork—a sort of "instant ruins."

Johnson's plans were met with some praise and some hostility, but the project was never begun and the funds appropriated never spent. The Ellis Island immigration Center continued to disintegrate.

Almost five years after the island was declared a national monument (although "ruin" would be a more accurate term), a group of militant Indians attempted to seize it to publicize the plight of their people. They were turned away by Park Service guards. Four months later, in July of 1970, members of the National Economic Growth and Reconstruction Organization (NEGRO) peacefully occupied the island. The goal of this non-profit group is to provide job opportunities for blacks and it has proposed turning Ellis Island into a work-and-rehabilitation center for drug addicts, welfare recipients and former convicts. NEGRO hopes to convert several of the buildings into factories for electronics assembly, chemical packaging, and other light industrial projects. The National Park Service has permitted the group to use the Ellis Island facilities for up to five years while the experiment continues.

A visitor to Ellis Island today needs an active imagination to be able to conjure up a vision of the throngs of bewildered immigrants who once poured out of barges and into the reception hall to be confronted by uniformed officials and guards. Now most of the buildings are deserted—decayed. Decades of neglect have, unfortunately, made the possibility of restoring the buildings and grounds extremely difficult and unlikely.

Armenian

But whatever the future of Ellis Island, its place in our history is secure. Coming by the millions, the immigrants often risked everything to live in the United States. They came from every European country and not a few African and Asian nations, borne along on a tide of hope which swept the world for almost half a century. Their hope was in America—American political and religious freedom and American wealth. Most of them never became rich and some were confronted with open hostility when they arrived, but very few gave up and returned to their former homelands. The buildings that these millions passed through have deteriorated almost beyond repair, and their fate remains undecided. But the buildings are only brick and iron, stone and wood. Called by some "Isle of Tears" and others "Island of Hope," Ellis Island's significance lies not in its physical structures, but in what it symbolized for the sixteen million who risked everything to come to a new land in search of a dream.

For if there is any story of Ellis Island, it is the story of the immigrants themselves.

Italian immigrants

Augustus F. Sherman Chief Clerk at Ellis Is. about 1890 — 1925 Photographs taken by him during his employment there.

Medical Examination Room

Hospital corridor

Baggage Waiting Room

Railroad Waiting Room

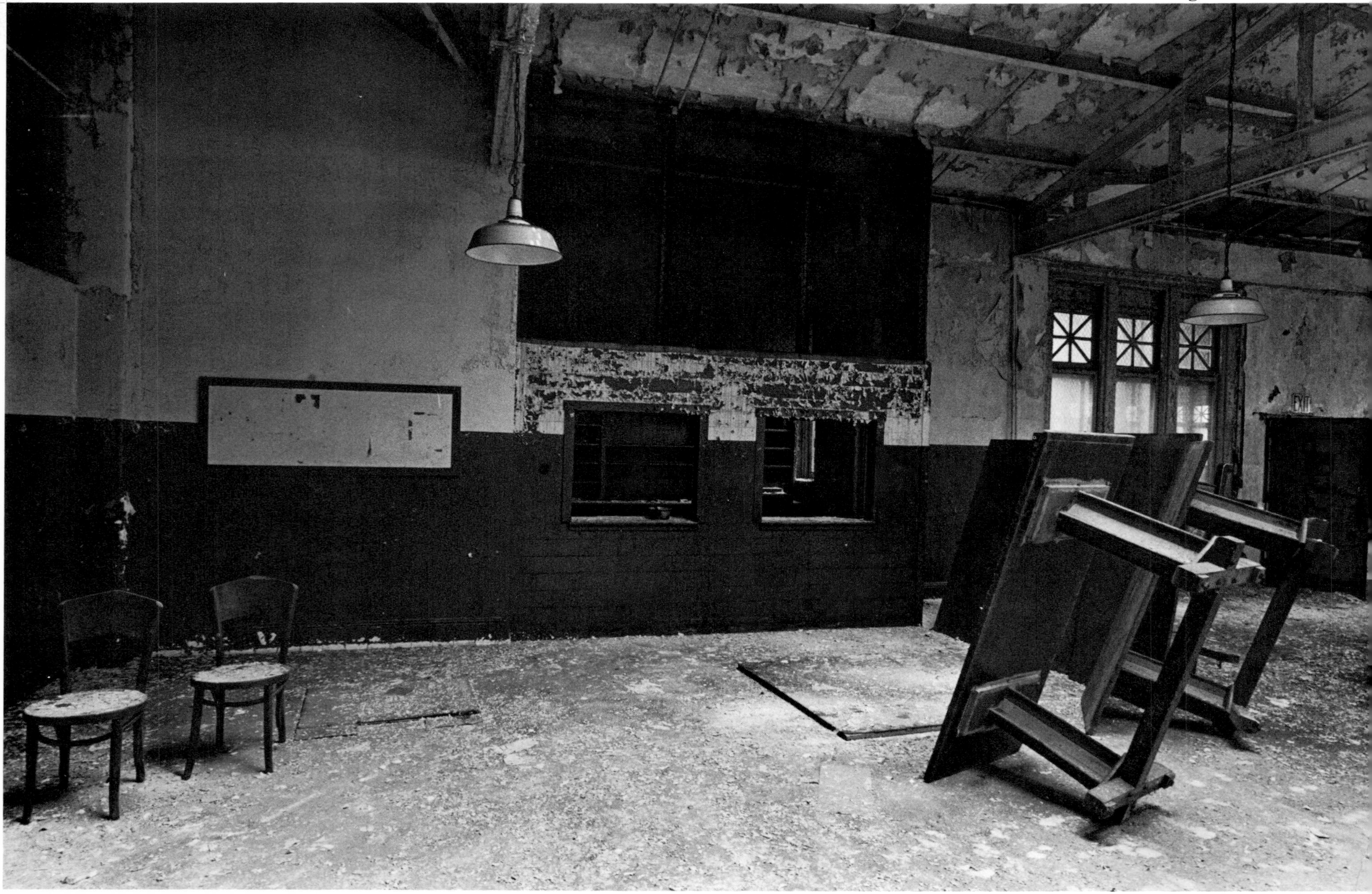

Inspector's desk

Coast Guard training aid

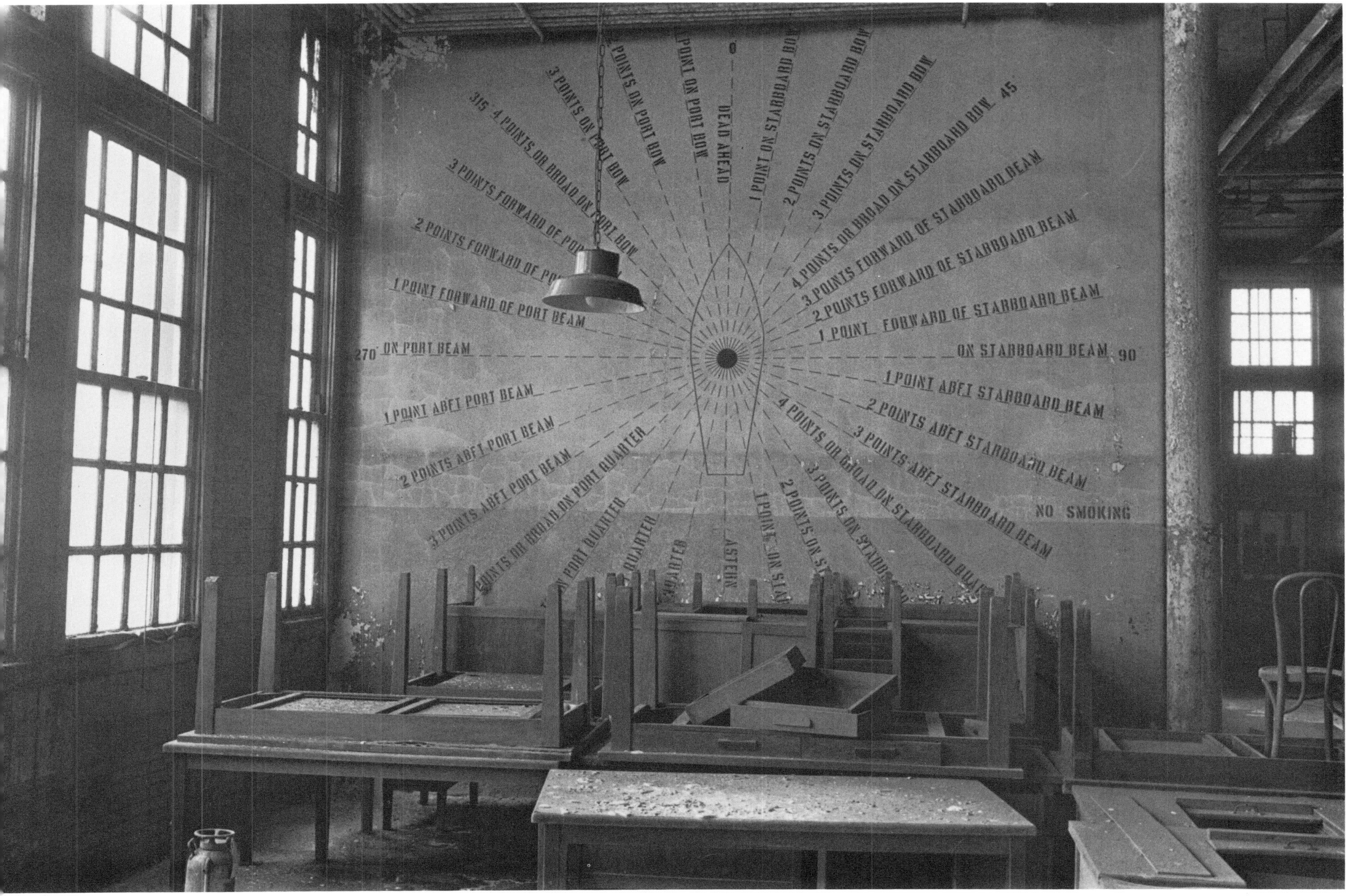

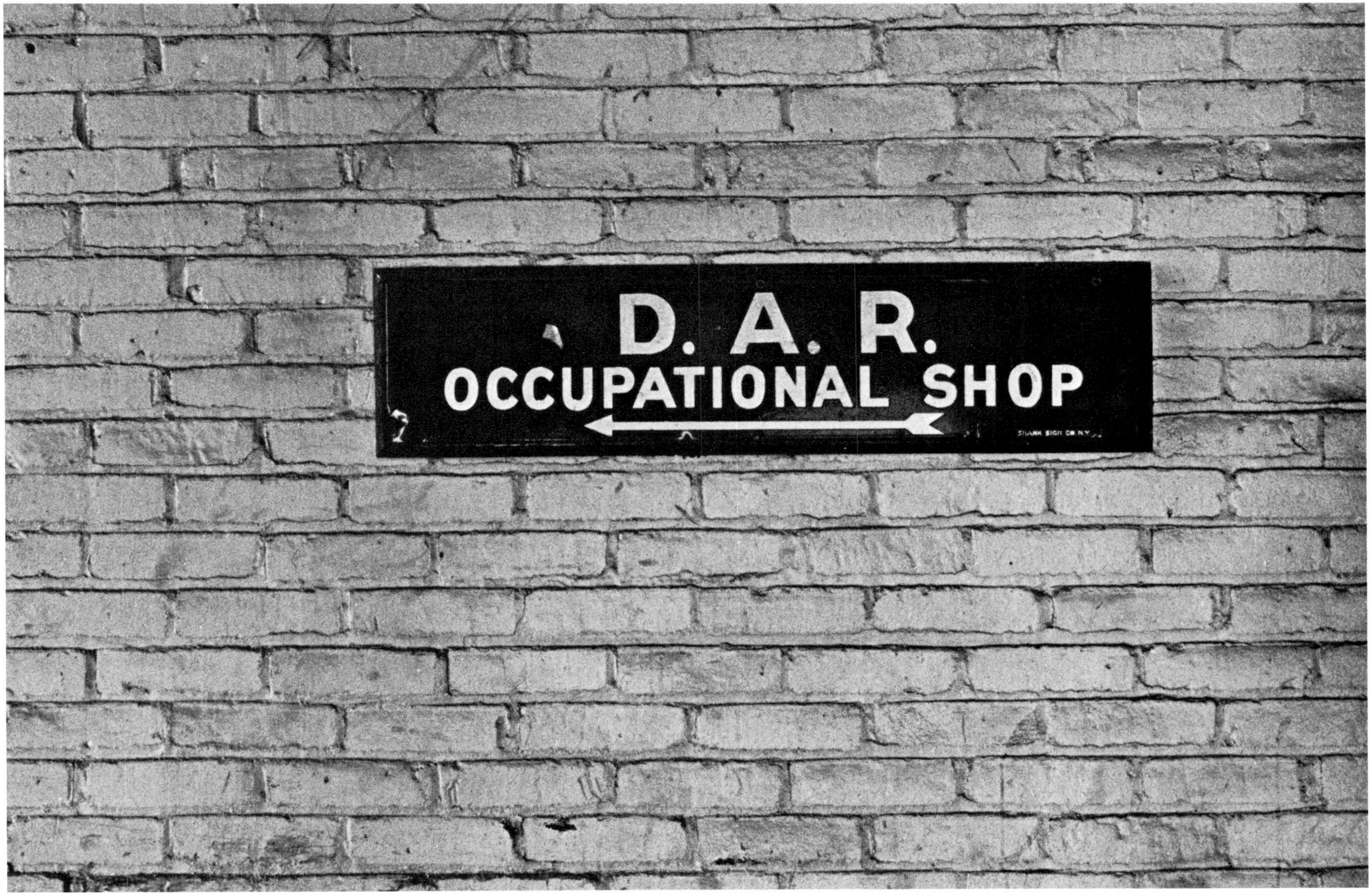
D. A. R.
OCCUPATIONAL SHOP

Medical Examination Room

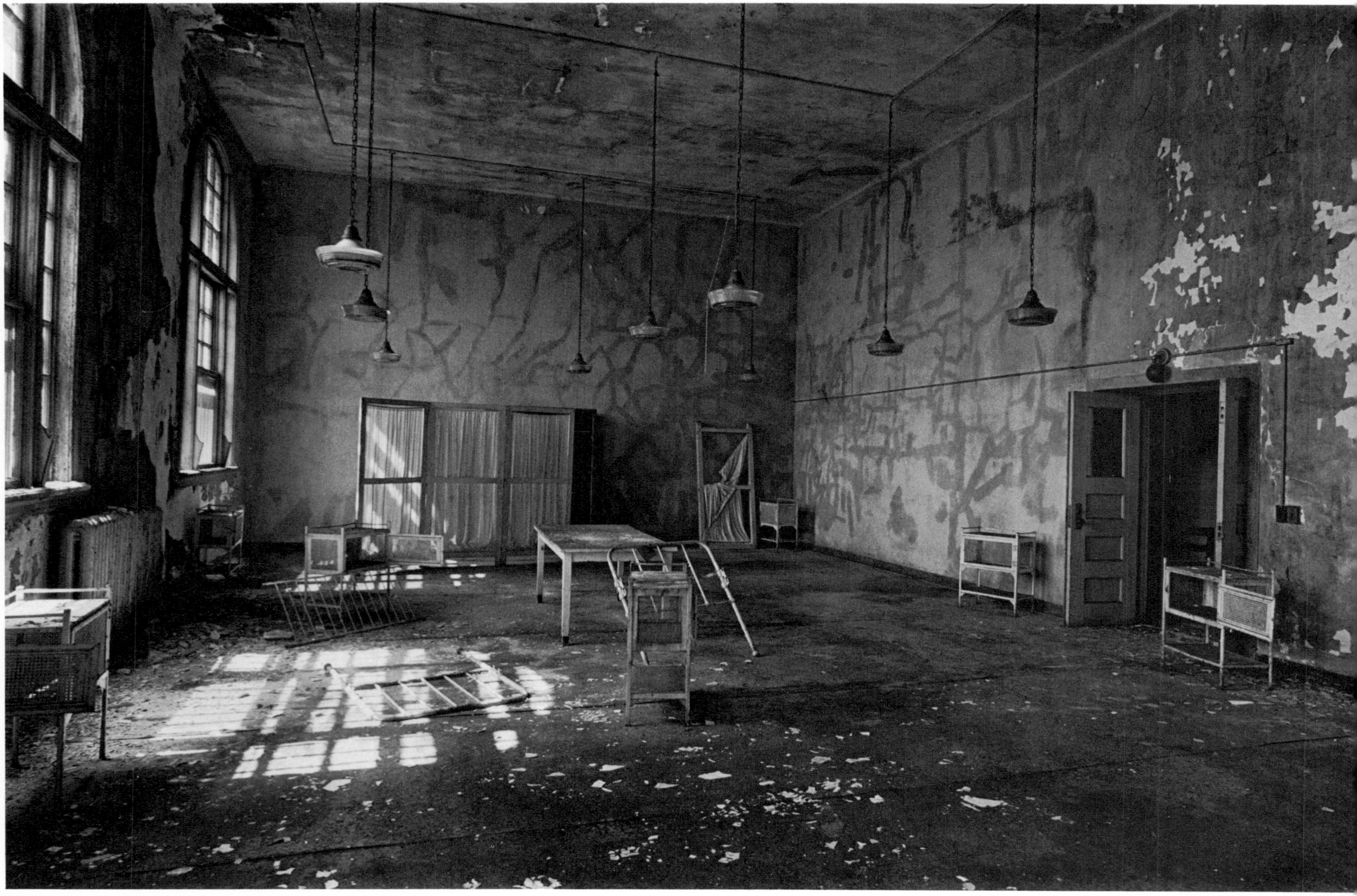

Morgue storage area

Coffee 3¢
Milk 6¢
2 Eggs 15¢
" with Bacon 22¢
"TONIGHTS SPECIAL"
SANDWICHES:
HAM 15¢
BLOOD TONGUE 13¢
HEAD CHEESE 13¢
GRUYÈRE CHEESE 14¢
CAMEMBERT " 14¢
PAY WHEN SERVED

Sheet presser

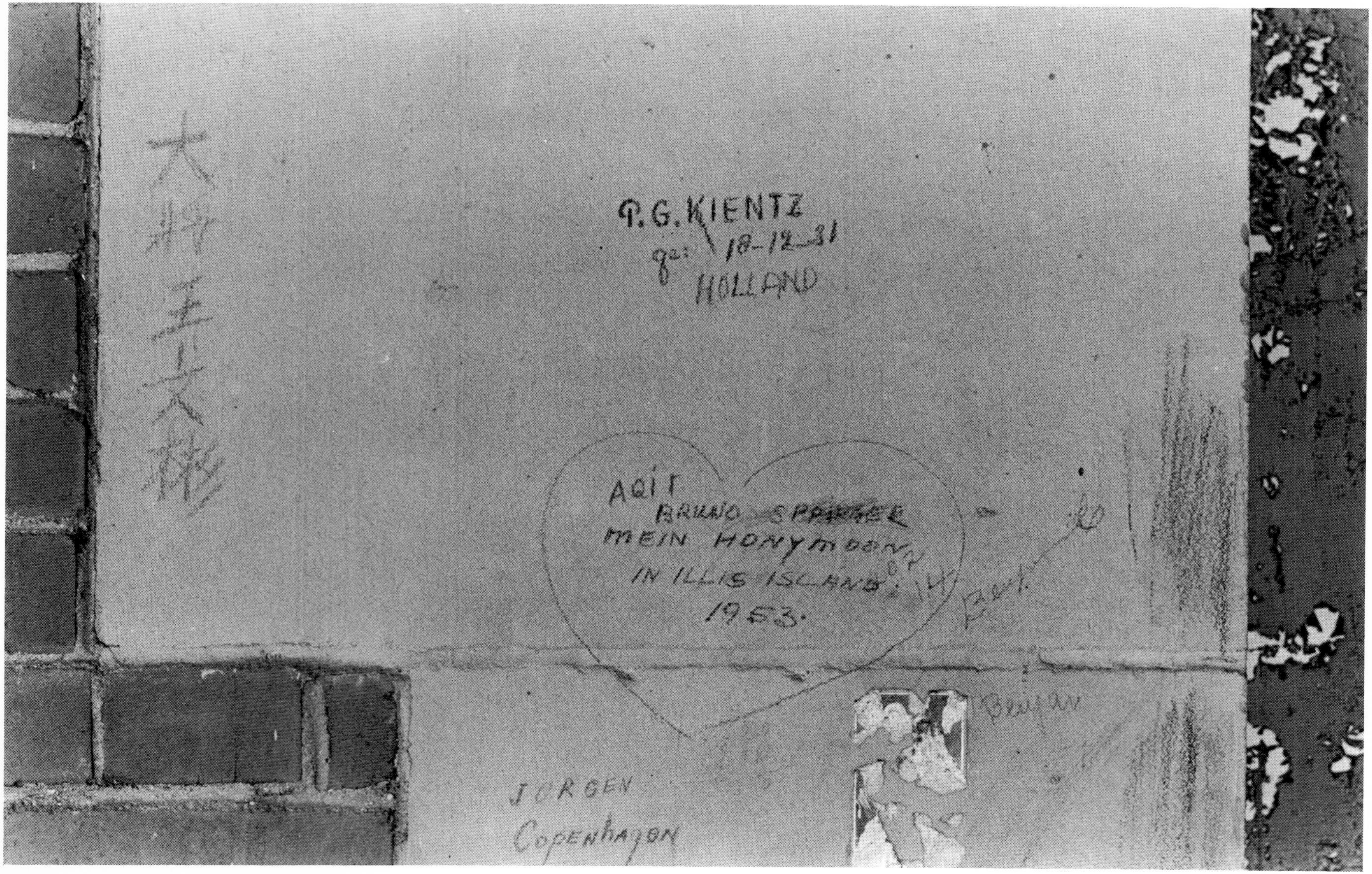
大将王文彬
P.G. KIENTZ
geb 18-12-31
HOLLAND
AQUI
BRUNO
MEIN HONYMOON
IN ILLIS ISLAND
1953
JORGEN
Copenhagen

Corridor used for school room

Corridor used for school room

INVENTORY 74

INVENTORY 1983